Masterpieces: Artists and Their Works

Michelangelo

by Shelley Swanson Sateren

Consultant:
Joan Lingen, Ph.D.
Professor of Art History
Clarke College
Dubuque, Iowa

Bridgestone Books
an imprint of Capstone Press
Mankato, Minnesota

Bridgestone Books are published by Capstone Press
151 Good Counsel Drive, P.O. Box 669, Mankato, Minnesota 56002
http://www.capstone-press.com

Library of Congress Cataloging-in-Publication Data
Sateren, Shelley Swanson.
    Michelangelo/by Shelley Swanson Sateren.
      p. cm.—(Masterpieces, artists and their works)
      Includes bibliographical references and index.
      Summary: Discusses the life, works, and lasting influence of Michelangelo.
      ISBN 0-7368-1125-7
      1. Michelangelo Buonarroti, 1475–1564—Juvenile literature. 2. Artists—Italy—
Biography—Juvenile literature. [1. Michelangelo Buonarroti, 1475–1564. 2. Artists.
3. Art appreciation.] I. Title. II. Series.
N6923.B9 S28 2002
709'.2—dc21
      2001003747

Editorial Credits

Blake Hoena, editor; Karen Risch, product planning editor; Heather Kindseth, cover and
    interior layout designer; Katy Kudela, photo researcher

Photo Credits

Art Resource/Scala, cover (right), 8, 12 (bottom)
Casa Buonarroti, Florence, Italy/Bridgeman Art Library, 6
Galleria dell' Accademia, Florence, Italy/Bridgeman Art Library, 12 (top)
Rome, Italy/Ken Welsh/Bridgeman Art Library, 18
San Pietro in Vincoli, Rome, Italy/Bridgeman Art Library, 20
Stock Montage, Inc., 4
St. Peter's, Vatican, Rome, Italy/Bridgeman Art Library, 10
Vatican Museums and Galleries, Vatican City, Italy/Bridgeman Art Library, cover (left),
    14 (top and bottom), 16

1 2 3 4 5 6 07 06 05 04 03 02

Table of Contents

Michelangelo and the Renaissance 5

Young Michelangelo 7

Apprenticeship 9

Pietà 11

Return to Florence 13

The Sistine Chapel 15

Working for the Popes 17

Saint Peter's Basilica 19

Michelangelo's Fame 21

Important Dates 22

Words to Know 23

Read More 23

Useful Addresses 24

Internet Sites 24

Index 24

Michelangelo is one of the most famous Renaissance artists.
He was skilled in sculpture, painting, and architecture.

Michelangelo and the Renaissance

Michelangelo Buonarroti (1475–1564) lived during the Renaissance. This period of European history lasted from the early 1300s to the late 1500s. During the Renaissance, Europeans rediscovered Greek and Roman ruins. In these remains, they found old writings and art.

People studied the Roman and Greek writings and art. These discoveries helped change people's opinions. Before the Renaissance, art mostly showed people's religious beliefs. During the Renaissance, art became a means of personal expression. People began to show their ideas through their artwork. They also began to collect and value art.

The Renaissance began in Italy. Many Roman ruins are found in this country. Raphael Sanzio, Sandro Botticelli, and several other Renaissance artists came from Italy. Michelangelo lived in a region of Italy called the Republic of Florence. This area was known for artists such as Leonardo da Vinci and Giovanni Bellini.

Madonna of the Stairs is one of Michelangelo's early sculptures. It is a bas-relief, carved from a flat surface.

Young Michelangelo

Michelangelo was born on March 6, 1475, in Caprese, Italy. His father, Lodovico, was the mayor of Caprese at the time. Michelangelo had three brothers.

Michelangelo's mother, Francesca, often was ill. She could not care for him. Lodovico sent him to stay with a stonecutter who lived near Caprese. Francesca died when Michelangelo was 6 years old.

The stonecutter's wife took care of Michelangelo. Michelangelo probably learned how to carve stone while living with the stonecutter. Later, sculpture would become his favorite type of art to create.

At age 10, Michelangelo moved to Florence with his family. His father sent Michelangelo to school to learn how to be a gentleman. He wanted Michelangelo to become a great military leader or politician.

But Michelangelo wanted to be an artist. At age 13, he became an artist's apprentice. Michelangelo worked and studied with the painter Domenico Ghirlandaio.

Michelangelo studied sculpture in Lorenzo de Medici's garden school. Later in life, Michelangelo carved this statue for the Tomb of Lorenzo de Medici.

Apprenticeship

Ghirlandaio taught Michelangelo fresco painting. Fresco artists painted directly on a fresh, wet plaster surface. The paint soaked into the plaster and kept its color.

Fresco painters first created drawings of their paintings called "cartoons." Apprentices traced the outline of the cartoons on the plaster with charcoal dust. Apprentices sometimes painted sections of the fresco. These sections usually were on parts of a wall or ceiling that were difficult to see.

Ghirlandaio thought that Michelangelo was a talented artist. He sent Michelangelo to see Lorenzo de Medici. Medici ruled Florence at the time. He also enjoyed art and supported artists.

Medici was impressed with Michelangelo's work. He invited Michelangelo to live at his palace and study with his sons. There, Michelangelo met many famous artists, poets, and scientists of the time. These people greatly influenced him and his ideas about art.

In 1499, Michelangelo finished *Pietà*. It is considered his first masterpiece.

Pietà

Michelangelo studied human anatomy. He learned how body parts fit together. He even gained permission to study dead bodies at a hospital. He cut the bodies open to learn where muscles and veins were located. This knowledge helped him create lifelike statues.

In 1492, Lorenzo de Medici died. Michelangelo decided to leave Florence shortly afterward. People had heard about his skills as a sculptor. He was invited to work in Rome. There, Michelangelo was hired to carve a statue of the Greek god of wine, Bacchus.

A church official saw Michelangelo's statue of Bacchus. He thought Michelangelo was a talented artist and hired him to carve a "pietà." This religious scene shows the Virgin Mary holding her dead son, Jesus Christ.

People were amazed at how lifelike Michelangelo's *Pietà* looked. The folds in the Virgin Mary's dress looked real. Her face seemed full of sadness as she held her son.

Michelangelo wanted to show David thinking about his battle with Goliath. In this statue, David seems to have a look of worry.

Return to Florence

Michelangelo's work in Rome had made him famous. Many people wanted to hire Michelangelo. In 1501, he decided to return to Florence. City officials in Florence hired Michelangelo to carve a statue. They had a tall block of marble for him to use.

Years before, a sculptor had begun to carve the biblical giant Goliath from this piece of marble. Some of his chisel marks are still on the back of Michelangelo's completed statue.

Michelangelo decided to carve a statue of David instead of Goliath. David is the religious hero who killed Goliath with a slingshot. A shed was built around the block of marble. Michelangelo then could work on the statue during bad weather and at night. It took him nearly three years to complete *David*.

At the time, most artists sculpted an image of David after he killed Goliath. But Michelangelo created a statue of David before the fight.

Michelangelo painted the Sistine Chapel's ceiling (above). Ezekiel (right) was one of the prophets he painted around the outer edge of the ceiling. People believed prophets could tell the future.

14

The Sistine Chapel

In 1508, Pope Julius II ruled the Roman Catholic Church. He asked Michelangelo to paint a fresco on the Sistine Chapel's ceiling. This church is in Rome. Michelangelo considered himself a sculptor, not a painter. But during the Renaissance, the pope was a powerful religious and political leader. Michelangelo had to follow his request.

The painting was difficult to complete. The Sistine Chapel's ceiling was nearly five stories high and more than 5,400 square feet (500 square meters). For four years, Michelangelo ate and slept little. His neck and back often hurt from looking up as he painted.

In 1512, Michelangelo finished the Sistine Chapel's ceiling. Nine panels down the center of the ceiling tell a biblical story. The first three panels show God creating the universe. The next three panels show Adam and Eve in the Garden of Eden. The last three panels show Noah and the flood. Michelangelo painted more than 300 human figures on the Sistine Chapel's ceiling.

Michelangelo painted some of the people in *The Last Judgement* to look like people he knew. He even painted a wrinkled image of himself toward the center of the painting.

Working for the Popes

Popes often asked Michelangelo to work for them. Pope Julius II asked him to make a tomb for him. Michelangelo carved the statue *Moses* for this burial place. Pope Leo X was Lorenzo de Medici's son. He asked Michelangelo to build a church and a library for the Medici family.

In 1536, Pope Paul III asked Michelangelo to paint the Sistine Chapel's back wall. This wall covers more than 2,000 square feet (185 square meters). Michelangelo took about six years to complete the painting *The Last Judgement*. This painting tells the story of the end of the world. Jesus Christ is shown surrounded by angels and saints. Below him, some people are rising toward heaven. Others are being pulled down to hell.

Michelangelo thought the human body was beautiful. He often created sculptures and paintings of nude people. Some church officials criticized *The Last Judgement* for this reason. They hired an artist to paint clothing on the figures in the painting.

Michelangelo spent the last 17 years of his life working on Saint Peter's Basilica. He designed the dome that covers the church.

Saint Peter's Basilica

In 1527, King Charles V of Spain attacked Rome. This attack weakened the pope's power. The people of Florence then rebelled against the pope's rule. They wanted to rule themselves. City officials asked Michelangelo to design the city's walls and gates to protect Florence. During the Renaissance, artists were expected to study architecture.

As he grew older, Michelangelo sculpted less. He was not as strong as he was in his youth. Carving stone became too hard for him. He spent most of his time painting, writing poetry, and designing buildings.

In 1547, Pope Paul III assigned Michelangelo to be the head architect of Saint Peter's Basilica in Rome. This church is considered the most important Catholic church in the world. Michelangelo was 72 years old when he started work on this project. Michelangelo did not accept any money for working on Saint Peter's Basilica. He believed it was his duty to God to do the work.

The Tomb of Pope Julius II is at the San Pietro in Vincoli (Saint Peter in Chains) church in Rome, Italy. The center statue is Michelangelo's *Moses*.

Michelangelo's Fame

Michelangelo died on February 18, 1564. He was 89 years old. He was buried at Santa Croce Church in Florence.

Michelangelo is famous for his work on the Sistine Chapel. In the 1980s, workers began to clean the church's ceiling. Many layers of dirt covered Michelangelo's painting. The workers took 10 years to finish.

Before the cleaning, people thought Michelangelo had used too many dark colors. The painting looked gloomy. But the cleaning showed that Michelangelo had used bright pinks, greens, and yellows in the painting.

Michelangelo is one of the world's most famous artists. His work influences many modern artists. They study his paintings and sculptures. They even learn how to create art by copying Michelangelo's works.

Today, people travel from all around the world to see Michelangelo's art. Tourists in Italy can see many of his famous sculptures. *David* is at the city art gallery in Florence. *Pietà* is at Saint Peter's Basilica in Rome.

Important Dates

1475—Michelangelo is born on March 6.

1481—Michelangelo's mother dies.

1485—Michelangelo's family moves to Florence.

1488—Michelangelo joins Ghirlandaio's workshop as an apprentice.

1489—Ghirlandaio introduces Michelangelo to Medici.

1492—Medici dies.

1499—Michelangelo finishes *Pietà*.

1501—Michelangelo begins work on *David*.

1508—Pope Julius II asks Michelangelo to paint the Sistine Chapel's ceiling.

1536—Michelangelo begins to paint *The Last Judgement*.

1547—Pope Paul III makes Michelangelo head architect of Saint Peter's Basilica.

1564—Michelangelo dies in Rome on February 18.

Words to Know

anatomy (uh-NAT-uh-mee)—the structure of a person's body
apprentice (uh-PREN-tiss)—someone who learns a trade or craft by working with a skilled person
architecture (AR-ki-tek-chur)—the designing of buildings
bas-relief (BAH-ree-LEEF)—a sculpture in which figures are carved or raised from a flat surface
fresco (FRESS-koh)—a painting made on a wet plaster surface; the paint soaks into the plaster and keeps its color.
Renaissance (REN-uh-sahnss)—a time of rebirth for art and learning that was inspired by ancient Roman and Greek ruins
ruins (ROO-ins)—the remains of something that has collapsed or been destroyed
tomb (TOOM)—a room or building that holds a dead body

Read More

Rebman, Renee C. *The Sistine Chapel.* Building History. San Diego: Lucent Books, 2000.
Stanley, Diane. *Michaelangelo.* New York: HarperCollins, 2000.
Tames, Richard. *Michelangelo Buonarroti.* The Life and Work of. Chicago: Heinemann Library, 2001.

Useful Addresses

Museum of Fine Arts, Boston
Avenue of the Arts
465 Huntington Avenue
Boston, MA 02115-5523

National Gallery of Canada
380 Sussex Drive
Box 427, Station A
Ottawa, ON K1N 9N4
Canada

Internet Sites

Cappella Sistina
http://www.christusrex.org/www1/sistine/0-Tour.html
Michelangelo Buonarroti (1475–1564)
http://www.michelangelo.com/buonarroti.html
WebMuseum, Paris—Michelangelo
http://www.oir.ucf.edu/wm/paint/auth/michelangelo

Index

apprentice, 7, 9
architecture, 4, 18, 19
Buonarroti,
    Francesca, 7
    Lodovico, 7
Florence, 5, 7, 9, 11, 13, 21

fresco, 9, 15
Ghirlandaio, Domenico, 7, 9
Medici, Lorenzo de, 8, 9, 11, 17
Renaissance, 4, 5, 15, 19
Sistine Chapel, 15, 17, 21